UNDER THE STARS OF TURTLE ISLAND

Under

the

Stars

of

Turtle Island

REBECCA DIETRICH

WAYFARER BOOKS

ABIQUIU, NEW MEXICO

WWW.WAYFARERBOOKS.ORG

Published in 2025 by Wayfarer Books
Cover Design and Interior Design by Connor Wolfe
TRADE PAPERBACK 9781965320297

10 9 8 7 6 5 4 3 2 1

Look for our titles in paperback, ebook, and audiobook wherever books are sold.
Wholesale offerings for retailers available through Ingram.

Wayfarer Books is committed to ecological stewardship.
We greatly value the natural environment and invest in conservation.

wayfarer@homeboundpublications.com
WAYFARERBOOKS.ORG

This book is dedicated to the Garden State
The land of Wawas and Pork Rolls
Springsteen Country
My home
New Jersey

TABLE OF CONTENTS

ACKNOWLEDGMENTS

"Brightest Flower." Poem. In *The Last Lullaby*. Bottlecap Press, 2024.

"Burning Snowflakes." *Mid-Atlantic Review* (April 2024).

"Collapse." *Steam Ticket* 26 (April 2023).

"Deer Woman." Poem. In *On Colonized Ground*. Alien Buddha Press, 2024.

"Dissociate." *The Hong Kong Review* 9, no. 2 (September 2024).

"Empty Cradle." *In Parenthesis* 8, no. 8 (July 2024).

"Futility." *Stockpot Literary Journal* (April 2024).

"Ghost." Poem. In *Under Her Eye: A Women in Horror Poetry Collection, Volume II*. Black Spot Books, 2023.

"Hexed." Poem. In *27th Annual Poetry Ink Anthology*. Philadelphia, PA: Moonstone Press, 2024.

"Historians Would Call Us Friends." *Oddball Magazine* (March 2023).

"MMIW." *Cool Beans Lit* 1 (September 2023).

"Moving On." *Burgeon Magazine* (March 2023).

"New Jersey Is My Home." *Burgeon Magazine* (March 2023).

"Ocean Waves." Poem. In *Sea or Seashore*. Wingless Dreamer Publisher, 2022.

"Paloma." Poem. In *The Last Lullaby*. Bottlecap Press, 2024.

"Reclaim." *Plumwood Mountain Journal* 9, no. 1 (September 2022).

"The Road to Dorothy." *Red Coyote* (November 2023).

"Shade." *Progenitor Art and Literary Journal* 59 (May 2024).

"Spring." Poem. In *Pull*. MOONLOVE Press, 2023.

"Sunset." *Red Coyote* (November 2023).

"Taken." Poem. In *S/He Speaks: Voices of Women and Trans Folx*. Moonstone Press, 2023.

"Tell Me How You Feel." *Havik: Cacophony* (May 2023).

"The Last Lullaby." Poem. In *The Last Lullaby*. Bottlecap Press, 2024.

"Unfair." *Making Waves: A West Michigan Review* no. 2 (September 2022).

"Your Memory Fades." *Havik: Cacophony* (May 2023).

THE ROAD TO DOROTHY

Along the road to Dorothy's realm,
Stands an abandoned farmhouse
Lost and forgotten,
by the railroad tracks
Its stands witness to battles fought.
Bullet casings scattered along the ground,
A blood streaked tub hides a darker past.
We painted the walls in palest white,
To match the haunted halls, alas,
Betrayal lurked within the foundation.
A decade of friendship lies entombed,
Hidden away within the crawl space's grasp.
To the fields we strolled,
where sunflowers weep,
There, from behind, treachery struck
For the love of a man,
name now faded,
But yours, oh yours,
still burns in memory.
Sisterhood's price,
an unwieldy cost,
Was he worth it?
The answer, unspoken.

TAKEN

A mother weeps.
Like many others before,
Her daughter has vanished.
Only memories remain,
As questions go unanswered.
A continuation
Of colonization.
Her fertile land,
Taken.
Her rich culture,
Taken.
Her bright child,
Taken.
Her short life,
Taken.

BALTIMORE

I thank you
For giving me reason
To write again,
Even if my tears
Wash the words away.
Somehow,
You turned Baltimore
Into a city of love
And my bed
Into a lonely place.
All I wanted
Was to love you,
Not learn a lesson.

UNFAIR

We asked for
A seat at the table.
So, when they refused,
We built our own
Now they claim
That it's unfair
Not to be included

YOUR MEMORY FADES

Like a sailing ship,
Disappearing out of sight,
Your memory fades.
Perhaps, it is for the best
Our love has been lost to time.

HEXED

In the dark void without your presence,
This curse you've woven tight around my core,
My heart suffocates, a captive essence,
Chasing shadows in the labyrinth of my mind's door.
I yearn for but a fleeting glance,
Through winding streets of my own design,
To caress your hair, a tender chance,
To behold those baby-blue eyes, divine.
Yet you fade, swallowed by the mist,
Enshrouded in the fog of my longing,
Since our first kiss, the catalyst,
No power, be it devil or savior, belonging.
Neither Satan's grasp nor Christ's embrace,
Can free me from your captivating spell,
Ensnared in your sorcery, I find no solace,
Bound to this dance, a tale only time can tell.

COLD

Your cold demeanor
Turns my fresh tears
Into icy snowflakes
Against my cheeks.
It was only yesterday,
You glowed with love.
What have I done
To make you change?

DEER WOMAN

Guardian to womenfolk,
She waits by the forest's edge,
With flowing black hair.
Should men be tempted,
Lured by her grace,
They'll face her secret,
No mortal is she,
A spirit of vengeance,
A daughter of care.
Beneath her beauty,
Hooves remain unseen,
When realization strikes,
It's too late to escape,
Their fate sealed,
For revenge, must be paid.

BROKEN PROMISE

"I will never
Fall in love again,"
Was a broken promise
When I met you.
Now I remember,
Why I swore it
In the first place.

BROKEN HEARTS

Can broken hearts
Be filled with love again,
Or will it only spill
Through the cracks
Like a shattered mug
Held together with tape?

MR. RADIO

I heard your voice through my radio.
Filled with melancholy, I sighed.
The tear stains remain on my heart.
I debate changing the station,
But I am frozen in place.
Trembling hands grip the steering wheel.
Your voice follows me everywhere.
It's hard to love the man on the radio,
It's even harder to forget him

SUNSET

I am like a sunset
Warm and full of beauty
Chasing the night sky
Just out of my reach

SPRING

When you held my hand,
I finally understood
Why birds sing
And build nests
In the warmth of spring,

YOU DESERVE TO BE HAPPY

I want your happiness,
Even if it lies
With another woman.
Devastated, I am,
Yet I bear the weight
Of my own conscience.
No pity, no apologies,
For you've done no wrong.
I admire your handling,
With grace and tender regard.
You're a worthy soul,
She's fortunate, indeed.
May your joy endure, my friend.

ANXIOUS

Dark overgrown roots
Peeking through red hair
Black eyeliner smeared
Under melancholy eyes
She waits by the door
For his return

MUSINGS

Crashing waves
Roar in my ears
As I sit on the jetty
Hugging my knees.
Is it ocean mist,
Or salty tears
I feel on my face?

AT THE SHORE

Hair as dark as driftwood
That's been washed ashore.
Skin the color of sand
On a sunny afternoon.
Eyes like pieces of sea glass
That glisten cerulean blue.
Even at the shore,
I still think of you.

TURTLE ISLAND

My roots run deep in this sacred land.
My ancestors lived and died here,
Long before the White man came.
"Our people met their people
when they got off the boat,"
As my grandfather used to say.
Yet we were the ones pushed around.
Gatsy was born in Georgia,
Her daughter Mahala in Oklahoma
And her daughter Buena too.
Grandpa Berry was born in Colorado
And my mother Nancy in Arizona.
She had me here in New Jersey.
When the time comes, I know
My children and their children
Will call Turtle Island home.

CASTAWAY

I once feared love's grasp,
"Bitter experience," I'd claim,
As if it held a curse,
To expel the ache and shame.
Yet, your lips met mine,
On that autumn's embrace,
And I found my misgivings,
A flawed sentiment to erase.
But fleeting was the joy,
My skies turned somber gray,
Adrift, I've felt since,
By your departure's disarray.

MOVING ON

I am over the worst of it.
Sorrow no longer calls my name,
But a piece of you remains
Deep inside my heart
As my life continues without you.

USED BOOKSTORE

I long for the musk
Of a used book store
Dust covered jackets
Crisp yellowed pages
Underneath my fingertips
As I search for secrets
Hidden within the binding

NEW JERSEY IS MY HOME

Home is where I feel sand between my toes
And smell freshly made boardwalk funnel cake
Sandcastles are washed away by the tide
Home is where the pine barrens stand tall
Ospreys soar above with their watchful gaze
As wildlife hides within reeds of cattails
Home is where the radio plays Springsteen
As I drive down the Garden State Parkway
To make my way back into your arms

PALOMA

My sweet unborn child,
Last night I had a dream.
I was cradling you in my arms,
But you vanished once I awoke.
When I close my eyes,
I can still see your dark hair
And your sleeping smile.
We will meet again someday.
I will make myself ready for you.

SUMMER HAZE

Amidst fields of lavender's grace,
Where dew-kissed earth meets my bare feet,
I yearn for the embrace of summer's haze,
A tranquil warmth, so pure and sweet.

HISTORIANS WOULD CALL US FRIENDS

She holds me in her arms
And I hold her in mine.
When I run my fingers
Across her soft skin,
Everything feels serene.

GASP

Her name
Echoes across the universe
As it escapes my lips.
Does she know
The air ceases to exist
Whenever she is near?

COLLAPSE

When the last drop of water is drunk,

The crops wither in their fields,

Lungs blacken from the falling ashes,

And the first innocent blood is spilled,

Will you still say it was worth it?

DISSOCIATE

Like an apparition
Divorced from my body
I pass through walls,
As if they were made of air.
Loved ones hold vigils for me
While I stand before them.
Veiled faces in mourning,
Do they not see me?
I'm not sure how I got here,
Or how I'm supposed to leave.

ENOUGH

Enough is enough,
It is you who left my side.
Stop your deceptive dance,
If you desire my presence,
Claim it without disguise.
I'm weary of your shrouded signs,
Either love me sincerely,
Or release me, leave me be.

OCEAN WAVES

I walk into the ocean
And I see the wave
Instead of running away
I face my fears head on
I cannot stop the tide
From coming in
So instead, I wait
For it to pass over me
I do not fear drowning
Only that I might
For the anticipation
Is far worse than reality

RECLAIM

They will never
Willingly give up
What they stole
From all of us.
We must claim
What belongs to us.
Make it their problem,
Not ours

TELL ME HOW YOU FEEL

If you wish me to disappear,
Then I shall fade into the mist
Like dew on a Sunday morning.
Don't let pleasantries lead me on
Down a path of false promised
But if you feel the same, my love,
Let it echo through the valleys
That fill my tender heart with doubt.

FIRE

Love is within the fire
That rages in the forest
Of a tender heart
Overgrown with sadness
Embers clear the way
For a new hope to emerge
From the darkest shadows
That linger on
After your absence

BURNING SNOWFLAKES

Radiation rains from above
Like burning snowflakes, it falls.
In awe of its beauty,
I reach out my hand.
The ash stains my palm,
Still warm to the touch.
If only I knew this was the end,
I would have done so much more.

THE LAST LULLABY

The world's final lullaby,
A melody bittersweet,
Where shooting stars dance,
But wishes find no retreat.

SILVER AND GOLD

Our love may not inspire bards to sing.
No beautiful princesses shall be rescued,
Nor shall brave knights quest for glory.
The sun will continue to rise in the east,
And set its evening glow upon the west.
No mountains will spring forth from the earth,
Nor will troubled seas part at our feet,
Should our tender lips embrace.
Our riches lie in the silver hair we grow,
And the golden years we spend as one.

LINGERING LOVE

Even within the tender grasp of love's embrace,

My mind's compass drifts back to you, unswayed.

Your presence lingers, an indelible trace,

In the depths of my thoughts, where memories wade.

LOVE IMMORTALIZED

The poems I crafted,

etched in books,

Stand on shelves,

timeless and still.

Within their pages,

tears unhooked,

Flow, as scholars and readers thrill.

Seeking meaning,

they dissect and explore,

Yet, my words,

they fall short, alas.

For the contours of your face,

I implore,

Hold a significance that words surpass.

My love for you ascends,

poetry aside,

Language falters,

unable to convey.

In your presence,

all words subside,

Lost in the depths where emotions stray.

BRIGHTEST FLOWER

You entered my life amidst the darkest hour,
Departing when shadows loomed so near.
Yet, strangely, you remain the brightest flower,
The best blessing that I hold dear.

FIRE AND WATER

In my youthful folly
I once thought of love like fire
Burning uncontrolled
With passion and flame
Now with life's wisdom
I know that love is like water
Quenching my thirst
With its soothing flow

CURSED

I was placed in this world
To love the unlovable.
Give me your heart
And I shall make it whole.
I am cursed to give
What I can never receive.
My love overflows for you,
While you dream of another.

IN SHADOWS, I HIDE

A love once within my grasp,
Now lies fallen in the grass.
What could I have done,
To halt the setting sun?
Once obtained, now lost,
A heart shattered by frost.
Perhaps, I yearned for more,
Than a soul could truly endure.
In shadows, I hide,
Feelings I cannot abide.

TREAD LIGHTLY

Your jealous gaze
Caught me by surprise,
As my hapless lover
unknowingly introduced us.
I understand, I do,
moving on is never easy.
However,
I don't seek your approval
to love again.
Let's lay our ghosts to rest
in the graves we dug for ourselves,
For our memories belong
to the shadows of the past.
Your once vibrant love,
left me wounded and scarred.
Tread lightly
with my newfound happiness,
Or summon the consequences
of your own undoing.

MMIW

My sisters,

lost in the veil of night,

Stolen by echoes of colonial might.

Pleas went unanswered,

a deafening void,

As men turned their gaze,

truth they avoid.

Now she exists as another name,

Blurred in the shuffle,

concealed by shame.

A fate shared with countless others found,

In a narrative woven on ancestral ground.

Missing,

murdered,

silenced in time,

Indigenous voices lost in genocide's crime.

FUTILITY

Two powers entwined,
their fierce dance unfolds,
The world watches closely,
their destiny foretold.
Nation against nation,
locked in an unyielding embrace,
Arms poised against arms,
no solace, no grace.
Bloodshed spawns more bloodshed,
a cycle unrestrained,
Families left in ruin,
their hopes forever stained.
Orphans' pleas for mercy,
echo through the haze,
Yet the victor's name eludes,
lost in the endless maze.
For who can govern a city of graves,
cold and still,
Where the echoes of tragedy resonate,
unfulfilled?
No ruler can emerge from this desolate domain,
Only grief and despair,
an everlasting refrain.

SHADE

One day, I will tell my children
I lived in the shadow of a great war.
My life always seemed veiled in darkness,
But little did I know,
I dwelled in the respite of shade.

GHOST

Your ghost haunts me
Even though
I'm the one who left
The rattle of the chains
You placed on my heart
Echoes in the night
I still see your face
With that deceiving grin
In my nightmares
Your lingering spirit
Lives on in my mind
Rest In Peace
For I am not

EMPTY CRADLE

For a fleeting moment,
You were the father of my child.
But fate wove other plans,
And once again, my womb lay barren –
A desolate, unwelcoming chamber.
How I longed to cradle in my arms
The gift of your firstborn,
But dreams, like whispers,
Are fickle and fleeting.

ABOUT THE AUTHOR

Rebecca Dietrich is a Cherokee poet and photographer from Atlantic City, New Jersey. Her debut chapbook *Scholar of the Arts and Inhumanities* (Finishing Line Press, 2023) won the Literary Titan Book Award for Poetry. She has also published *The Last Lullaby* (Bottlecap Press, 2024) and *On Colonized Ground* (Alien Buddha Press, 2024). Dietrich's poetry has been published in *Red Coyote*, *Havik*, *Steam Ticket*, and elsewhere. She holds a B.A. in Psychology with a minor in Holocaust & Genocide Studies from Stockton University.

You can follow her on Instagram
@limericks_and_asphodels.

At Wayfarer Books we believe poetry is the language of the earth. We believe words—shaped like rivers through wild places—can change the shape of the world. We publish poets and writers and renegades who stand outside of mainstream culture—poets, essayists, and storytellers whose work might withstand the scrutiny of crows and coyotes, those who are cryptic and floral, the crepuscular, and the queer-at-heart. We are more than just a publisher but a community of writers. Our mission is to produce books that can serve as a compass and map to all wayfarers through wild terrain.

wayfarerbooks.org

www.ingramcontent.com/pod-product-compliance
Lightning Source LLC
Chambersburg PA
CBHW030515130626
46549CB00007B/3007